●Fun with English●

Horrors & Howlers

How not to misuse English

Norman Barrett
Illustrated by Peter Stevenson

Chambers

Editor: John Grisewood

Illustrations: Peter Stevenson
(Kathy Jakeman Illustration)

CHAMBERS
An imprint of Larousse plc
Elsley House, 24-30 Great Titchfield Street,
London W1P 7AD

First published by Chambers 1995

2 4 6 8 10 9 7 5 3 1

Illustrations copyright © Larousse plc 1995
Text © Norman Barrett 1995

A CIP catalogue record for this book is available
from the British Library.

ISBN 0 550 325107

Printed in Spain

Contents

1 What's the point of punctuation?

You have probably never come across a sentence where the same word follows itself ten times. Here's an example: Harry who where Hannah had had had had had had had had had had had where Hannah had had had. Doesn't make any sense, does it? But if you add some punctuation — commas and quotation marks — you might begin to see what it means: Harry, who, where Hannah had had 'had had' had had 'had', had had 'had had' where Hannah had had 'had'.

You see, Harry and Hannah had taken a grammar test at school. It was all about verbs and tenses. In the answer to one question, Harry had written: 'I had a white face because I had had a fright.' Whereas Hannah had put down, in answer to the same question: 'I had had a white face because I had used too much powder.' So, where Hannah had had 'had had' Harry had had 'had' and so on.

This, in a rather absurd way, shows how important punctuation is when you are writing. In writing you often use commas where, in speech, you would probably pause — as in this sentence.

Punctuation marks help the reader to understand clearly what you've written.

If you got the sentence in the box right, you would have used a capital letter, some commas, an apostrophe and a question mark, as well as putting spaces between the words. Shouldn't there be a full stop at the end of every sentence? No, you do not use a full stop when you have a question mark at the end of a sentence, as you can see in the last sentence. And you don't use one with an exclamation mark either!

The cat and the comma
There is a riddle which asks: What's the difference between a cat and a comma? The answer is that a cat has its claws at the end of its paws, while

Pussy, please pause!

See if you can rewrite this sentence
afterallifyouwrotewith-
outspacesbetweenwords-
forexampleitwouldbevery-
difficultforthereadertofol-
lowwouldntit
(answer on page 26)

In the following examples, some commas are needed and some should not be there, or perhaps the sentence is OK as it stands. What do you think? See the answers page 26 to find out how many you got right.

1 Jack my youngest brother has just started school.
2 Schoolteacher, Hilary Humperdinck, was arrested for dangerous driving.
3 The race was sponsored by, but not connected with the department store.
4 As soon as the rain started up went the umbrellas.
5 The primary colours are red, blue, and yellow.
6 You heard me calling but you did not answer.
7 The senator, born in Orlando, Florida of poor parents supported the scheme.
8 The hand that rocks the cradle, rules the world.
9 Having had lunch I went back to my office.
10 'Here I am,' Tom replied.

The hand that rocks the cradle ...

a comma has its pause at the end of its clause.

Commas are the most commonly used punctuation marks, and one of their uses is to separate clauses in a sentence. The comma in the last sentence does just that, after the word 'marks'. There is no strict rule about this, and some writers prefer not to use a comma before 'and'. For example, you might write: 'My new car is red and has a radio.' The two clauses are short and have the same subject ('My new car'), so a comma is not necessary.

In such cases a comma is often a matter of preference or style. Sometimes a comma is essential. Take this sentence: 'When the ball was over the moon, which had been hidden by clouds, finally came out.' You cannot help misreading this because it does not have an all-important comma, which should go after the word 'over'. Then you will realize that the 'ball' referred to is a 'dance'.

Would you like a pocket calculator?

Comma sense

You can usually tell where to put a comma, because there would be a natural pause — sometimes just a slight one — if you were speaking or reading, as in: 'Harrison Ford, the American film star, made a surprise appearance.' You would not put commas in this: 'British hurdler Sally Gunnell won the world 400 metres title.' But you would if it were phrased this way: 'A British hurdler, Sally Gunnell, won the ....'

Commas may also be used to separate direct speech: Dan replied, 'I am not sure what to do about the computers'. But there is no reason for using a comma between a house number and a street in addresses.

Dash it — use a hyphen

Uncle: 'Would you like a pocket calculator for your birthday, Jack?' Jack: 'No thanks, uncle. I already know how many pockets I have.' In this little joke, Jack was being funny. But if there were such a thing as a calculator for counting pockets, it would probably be spelt with a hyphen: pocket-calculator. The hyphen is one of those little dashes we use in compound words — that is, words made up from two or more other words. Examples are: all-important and vice-captain. It is also used when a prefix is added to a word beginning with a capital letter: anti-Europe, un-American.

Compound words

There is no simple 'rule' for the use of hyphens. Compound words usually start out as two separate words, such as 'gate post'. As a combination of words becomes more familiar, a hyphen may be inserted (gate-post), and finally the compound may become one word (gatepost). This

process could take place over scores of years. Different dictionaries often give different versions of the same compound. Compound words with hyphens are common in British English. In American English, compounds are usually one word or two separate words

Multi-word phrases describing a following noun usually require hyphens:

a first-class novel
but *This novel is first class.*
But beware the common mistake: *a badly-made jacket.*
Badly cannot possibly describe *jacket,* so the hyphen in such cases is wrongly used.

It's right, its wrong

One mark that seems to cause a lot of trouble is the apostrophe. It shouldn't do, because it's not really difficult to use, and one of its main uses is made clear in this very sentence. This is as a replacement for a letter that is dropped when a word is shortened, as in 'shouldn't' for 'should not' and 'it's' for 'it is'. The word 'its', as in 'its main uses', has a different meaning and doesn't have an apostrophe.

Here are some words that developed out of two or more separate words. Can you say what the original words were in each case? (answers on pages 26 and 27)

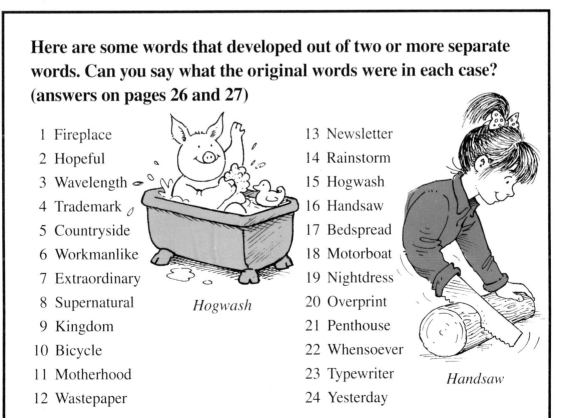

1 Fireplace
2 Hopeful
3 Wavelength
4 Trademark
5 Countryside
6 Workmanlike
7 Extraordinary
8 Supernatural
9 Kingdom
10 Bicycle
11 Motherhood
12 Wastepaper

13 Newsletter
14 Rainstorm
15 Hogwash
16 Handsaw
17 Bedspread
18 Motorboat
19 Nightdress
20 Overprint
21 Penthouse
22 Whensoever
23 Typewriter
24 Yesterday

Hogwash

Handsaw

A common blunder in writing is to put an apostrophe in 'its'. All you need to remember is that 'it's' means 'it is'. Otherwise, it should be spelt 'its'.

Which of the following are wrong?

(answers on page 27)

1 Its a lovely day today.

2 Its raining in my heart.

3 Its not fair.

4 Its only drawback is the weather.

5 When it's raining, it's raining violets.

Possessive apostrophes

Another use of the apostrophe is with an 's', to show belonging, as in 'Kylie's hair'. There is no problem here. When used with a plural word, the apostrophe goes after the 's', as in 'the boys' books'. (If the books belonged to just one boy, though, you would write 'the boy's books'.) Plurals without an 's', such as 'men', take the apostrophe before an 's' — 'men's clothing'. When a name ends with an 's', you usually add an apostrophe before another 's' — 'Jones's brother', 'Frances's pen'. But you would write or say 'Mr Masters' hat', not 'Mr Masters's hat', which would sound odd.

All these 'belonging' words with apostrophes are called possessives.

Some possessives do not have apostrophes, such as his, hers, theirs and mine.

Raining violets

Try correcting the following examples, which have missing or misplaced apostrophes (answers on page 27):

1 Thats my sisters poem.

2 Youll let me know, wo'nt you?

3 Is that ball yours'?

4 No, its Jonese's.

5 Your's sincerely.

6 Womens' rights.

7 The mens room.

8 Its a hard life.

9 I didnt want to do it.

10 Are'nt you lucky?

2 Misprints

'Red squirrels have reddish-brown backs with white underpants.' The typist should have typed 'underparts', but this misprint did not get published. An editor spotted it and corrected it — the spoilsport.

Before books, magazines or newspapers are printed and published, the writing is usually checked by proof-readers to correct any mistakes in the 'copy', as the original writing is called. In modern times, if the copy is set on a word processor, the spelling can easily be checked automatically by the computer.

Even so, blunders still get through, especially in newspapers, where copy must be processed in a hurry. And even a computer would not have caught the 'underpants' error, because the misprint was a word in its own write (sorry, that should be 'right'). For the same reason, 'Pope stars in drugs scandal' (for 'Pop stars ...) would also beat the computer.

Quite often, people make mistakes because their mind plays little tricks – 'underpants' is a more common word than 'underparts', for example. And what about this, from a report of a school soccer match in a local paper: 'Billy scored a beautiful goat from a narrow angle.' The name 'Billy' obviously suggested 'goat'.

Some misprints can be embarrassing, as a local paper found when they advertised, in large bold letters, for a 'SCUTINEER', whose job would be to check the spelling of adverts

placed in the paper. They certainly demonstrated their need for a 'scrutineer', as it should be.

More misprints on the next page.

White underpants

Majority of Illterates Live in the Third World

Newspaper headline

The following all contain one misprinted word. See if you can correct them (answers on page 27):

1 The sour milk is hung for several hours in a muslim cloth.
2 All you could see at the end of the table was a large bore with apple in mouth.
3 The ship was edged off the rocks by two thugs.
4 The express was in collision with a good train.
5 The clown tripped and hurt his fool on the wall.
6 The diner asked for a glass of waiter.
7 You can tell it's dawn when the clock crows.
8 The game was watched by a huge crow in the stands.
9 A salon is a lounge or deception room.
10 The islanders were much feared Satin worshippers.
11 In the dark her face was almost risible.
12 He picked up his ears at the mention of a walk.

A huge crow

A large bore with apple in mouth ...

3 How not to spell potatoe

By the time you get to the end of this sentence, you should have spotted three seperate mispellings, apart from the one in the chapter heading. You can find out what they are by looking in the answers on page 27. English spelling is not easy. Words are not always spelt as they sound. And there is often more than one way of spelling words that sound the same.

Sounds the same

The words 'sight' and 'site' sound the same but, as you can see, they are spelt differently, and they also have different meanings. 'Sight' is something you see or the sense that you see with. 'Site' is a place for a building. Such pairs of words are called 'homophones'. This pair, sight and site, have another homophone, pronounced the same. Do you know what it is and what the word means? (answer on page 27)

It's fun finding homophones. Another example of a triple one, with words beginning with three different letters, is: air (atmosphere), ere (before), and heir (someone who inherits). You can add to this with e'er (a contraction of 'ever') and eyre (a circuit of a travelling judge). If we count proper names — of places or people — there is Ayr (town in Scotland) as well as surnames such as Ayer and Ayre.

The following are clues to pairs (or triples) of homophones — for example, 'a portion' and 'no fighting' would be 'piece' and 'peace'. See how many you can solve (answers on page 27):

1   A goes on the finger, B means to squeeze water out.
2   A is what a monarch does, B comes from clouds, C is used to guide a horse.
3   A is the whole, B is just part.
4   A is expensive, B what a stag is.
5   A is a number, B the past tense of eat.
6   A is 24 sheets of paper, B a group of singers.
7   A is prohibited, B a group of musicians.
8   A is what trees are made of, B shows willing.
9   A is to carry, B means naked.

Prohibited musicians

(continued on next page)

MISSPELLINGS

(continued on from page 11)
(answers on pages 27 and 28)

The officer is a bit of a nut

The missing lynx

10 A is a young male, B floating mark.

11 A is to colour, B to pass away.

12 A is a wharf, B opens doors.

13 A is a collar, B is not smooth.

14 A is a hint, B to wait in line.

15 A is an officer, B is found in a nut.

16 A is ordinary, B a flat surface.

17 A is animal hair, B a tree.

18 A is nil, B lives in a convent.

19 A is not wrong, B what you do on paper, C is a ritual,
    D a maker (usually used in compound words).

20 A is a lord, B juts out to sea.

21 A is a cat-like animal, B is where golf is played.

22 A is a church corridor, B is land surrounded by water.

23 A is an American coin, B is a smell.

24 A is this place, B is to listen.

25 A is a frog-like animal, B is to be pulled along.

One last trick question: What is a 'Playwrite'?

Spelling rules

English has developed over hundreds of years from many different languages, and this is why spelling seems to be so haphazard. But there are some rules of spelling that help. A good one is: 'i' before 'e' except after 'c'. This tells you that when the letters 'i' and 'e' are used together to give the vowel sound as in 'grief' or 'brief', the 'i' comes first - unless the sound comes after the letter 'c', as in 'deceive'.

There are plenty of words that follow this rule, such as believe, relieve and siege, and conceive, receive and ceiling. But there are usually exceptions to spelling 'rules'. The few exceptions to this rule include 'seize'. A common mistake is to spell it 'sieze' to follow the rule. Words such as 'being' and 'beige' do not break the rule because they have different vowel sounds.

'-able' or '-ible'? Why quibble?

The spelling of words ending in '-able' or '-ible' not surprisingly causes endless confusion. After all,

Good boy, 'Fetch'

See if you can spot the misspelt words in the following and correct them (answers on page 28):

1 Deciet
2 Achieve
3 Seeing
4 Thier (belonging to them)
5 Wier (dam across a river)
6 Casheir
7 Cavalier
8 Musketier
9 Sieve
10 Seismic (to do with an earthquake)
11 Retreiver
12 Shreik

why should it be 'lovable' but 'legible', 'desirable' but 'flexible'? There is no easy answer. It depends whether the words have come from French, Latin or English roots. But that's no help when you are trying to spell a word. Sometimes, you can tell by the sound of the word how it should be spelt. But often the only way to avoid a mistake is to look up the word in a dictionary. And when you see one of these words in a book or newspaper, make a mental note of the spelling.

You might be wondering whether all this is worth the effort. Certainly, it is not a criminal offence to write '-ible' where you should write '-able'. And it is well known that people can reach the highest office in government, for example, without being able to spell a simple word like 'potato'.

We should all take a pride in our language, but is correct spelling an important factor in writing good English? What do you think?

Just add an 's'

One of the simplest rules of spelling is when you want to make a word plural, you usually just add an 's' - cat/cats, station/stations, apple/apples and so on. But, as always, there are many exceptions.

Potato is one of them. You make it plural by adding 'es' — potatoes. It is the same for other words ending in 'o'. You add 'es' to make heroes and buffaloes. So you would expect the plural of 'zero' to be 'zeroes', but it isn't. It's 'zeros'. Unfortunately, you have to learn the plurals for words ending in 'o'. It's the only sure way.

Double trouble

Another common error is to double a letter at the end of a verb when using a word formed from it, such as 'benefitted' instead of 'benefited', or doing the reverse, such as 'traveling' instead of 'travelling' (although 'traveling' is the correct American spelling).

Many misspellings occur because people are confused by the sound of words, often when they are not properly pronounced. So 'library' might be wrongly spelt as 'libary', 'laboratory' as 'labratory'. And, of course, some words are just maddeningly difficult to spell!

What are the plurals of the following?
(answers on page 28):

1 banjo
2 mosquito
3 cargo
4 dynamo
5 halo
6 motto
7 tornado
8 tomato
9 soprano
10 volcano
11 echo
12 ratio

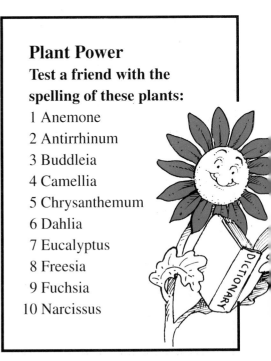

Plant Power
Test a friend with the spelling of these plants:
1 Anemone
2 Antirrhinum
3 Buddleia
4 Camellia
5 Chrysanthemum
6 Dahlia
7 Eucalyptus
8 Freesia
9 Fuchsia
10 Narcissus

Most of the following words are misspelt. With the help of your *Chambers Dictionary* see if you can pick these out and correct them (answers on pages 28 and 29):

1	abbreviate	26	conscience	51	imobile	76	occured
2	absess	27	dachsund	52	impessario	77	oddysey
3	abyss	28	deciduous	53	indefensable	78	parrafin
4	acellerate	29	deliccatessen	54	inocuous	79	pavilion
5	accomodate	30	desicate	55	inuendo	80	preferrence
6	acquire	31	diarrhea	56	intersede	81	propellor
7	adress	32	dinghy	57	interogate	82	questionaire
8	allotted	33	extasy	58	irrasible	83	rarify
9	annoint	34	eczema	59	irridescent	84	rennaisance
10	artic	35	embarass	60	isoceles	85	ressurection
11	assasin	36	Fahrenhiet	61	jodphurs	86	sacharrin
12	bargin	37	fidjeting	62	kharki	87	sacriligious
13	barly	38	flite	63	kichin	88	sandwich
14	braggadocio	39	focussed	64	laquer	89	saphire
15	brocolli	40	fuselage	65	lassoo	90	satisfactry
16	bullrush	41	gasious	66	liase	91	saxaphone
17	calander (of days)	42	gaity	67	liquify	92	speciman
18	caress	43	grammer	68	locquacious	93	spheracal
19	catarh	44	grievious	69	mayonaise	94	supercede
20	cauliflower	45	gymhkana	70	milennium	95	symetry
21	chihuahua	46	hankerchief	71	mispelled	96	tempory
22	colloquial	47	harrass	72	mocassin	97	tomatoe
23	collonade	48	herbacious	73	monastry	98	tyrrany
24	collossal	49	hundreth	74	neice	99	vermillion
25	conceed	50	hypocricy	75	nucular	100	yahct

4 Is that really what they said?

'Lead on, Macduff.' How often have you heard someone say that? It is usually a jokey way of asking someone to go first. Most people who say it probably know it comes from Shakespeare's play Macbeth. *But what they do not realize is that it is a misquote. What Macbeth says is 'Lay on, Macduff' — a challenge to fight.*

Quotes from famous writers, leaders and wits are quite useful in writing or speaking if you want to make a particular point. But it helps to get them right.

Many of the everyday phrases and sayings we use are from the Bible or Shakespeare or some other source. We may not realize it, because they have become part of the language. When someone talks about 'blood, sweat and tears', meaning enormous effort and sacrifice, they think they are quoting from one of the famous speeches made by Winston Churchill, the great British leader in the Second World War. But what he said was: 'I have nothing to offer but blood, toil, tears and sweat.'

Play it again Sam

Another famous misquote is 'peace in our time'. Most people believe that this is what British prime minister Neville Chamberlain said after signing an agreement with German dictator Adolf Hitler before that war. But it comes from the Book of Common Prayer. What Chamberlain said was: 'I believe it is peace for our time.' You could say that a little knowledge is a dangerous thing. Or, more correctly, a little learning is a dangerous thing.

I want to be alone

Can you correct the following altered quotes from famous people or books (answers on page 30):

1 Let there be night. (The Bible)

2 When shall we four meet again ...? (*Macbeth*, Shakespeare)

3 On the waters of Gitche Gumee. (*Hiawatha's Childhood*, Longfellow)

4 Warriors of the world unite. (Karl Marx)

5 I don't want to belong to any club that won't have me as a member. (Groucho Marx)

6 The report of my death was an error. (Mark Twain)

7 Mr Livingstone, I presume. (Henry Morton Stanley)

8 If you can meet with Victory and Disaster and treat those two impostors just the same. (*If*, Rudyard Kipling)

9 Tiger! Tiger! burning bright in the stillness of the night ... (*Songs of Experience*, William Blake)

10 The law is an ass. (Mr Bumble in *Oliver Twist*, Charles Dickens)

11 Water, water, everywhere, and not a drop to drink. (*The Ancient Mariner*)

12 They shall not grow old as we who are left grow old. (Laurence Binyon)

13 I want to be alone. (Greta Garbo)

14 Play it again Sam. (Humphrey Bogart in the film *Casablanca*)

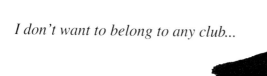

I don't want to belong to any club...

5 Rules of grammar? Ignore them!

The presenter of a radio phone-in programme about grammar asked the listeners to 'ring in and let me know some of the obvious grammatical errors that we're guilty'. In doing so, he made a pretty bad one himself. Grammatically, his sentence did not make sense. He should have said '... guilty of'. Perhaps he was trying to avoid making what he thought was a grammatical error himself — ending a sentence with a 'preposition'.

'Preposition' is a long word for some of the shortest words in the English language – of, in, on, at, by, up, to, for, off and so on. And prepositions are among the most misused words in the language. But there is no reason why you shouldn't end a sentence with one.

This so-called 'rule' of grammar never has made sense and is responsible for people getting into all sorts of contortions in both speech and writing. A preposition usually goes before the word or group of words it applies to, but it does not have to. The sentence 'That's the house in which I now live', could equally well be written 'That's the house I now live in'.

A common blunder is to use an extra preposition when you have already used one, as in the Beatles song that includes the line: 'This ever-changing world in which we live in.'

Different from or than
What prepositions to use after the words 'different', 'compare' and 'centre' is the cause of much argument. (Well, some people get hot under the collar over such matters!) There are no simple rules, and the choice depends on what comes after the preposition.

Try changing the following sentences without making them sound ugly or unnatural. Bet you can't.

What are you getting so angry about?

He saved every bottle-top he could lay his hands on.

It doesn't matter what they are eaten with.

That was disgraceful behaviour, whatever rules you were brought up by.

The refugees had nowhere to go to.

Up

Over

Down

According to most grammar books, 'different' should be followed by 'from' in both British and American English: 'Cats are different from dogs.' But, in practice, 'different to' (mainly British use) and 'different than' (American) are commonly used. 'Different than' is quite acceptable in a sentence such as: 'The garden is different than it was last year.' A possible alternative would be: 'The garden is different from what it was last year', a cumbersome sentence indeed. 'Different to' sometimes sounds better than 'different from' and there is no reason to avoid it, especially in speech. But it should always be 'differs from' and 'the difference between'.

Compared with and to

There is a difference between 'compare with' and 'compare to'. The first, which is the more common, is used to compare things side by side, noting differences or similarities, as in: 'Compared with cycling, swimming is better for exercising the arms.' Comparing something or someone 'to' is to liken it to, as in the opening of one of

Shakespeare's sonnets: 'Shall I compare thee to a summer's day?'

'Their social life centred round the bingo hall.' The use of 'centre round' instead of 'centre on' is frowned upon, mainly because it is not physically possible. But this does not matter in language. Few idioms are logical – try 'standing on ceremony', for example. 'Centre round' is now commonly used, and is accepted even in the best of circles!

Find the preposition

See if you can find a suitable preposition from the list given to fit into the following phrases (answers on page 30):

1 .... a mess.
2 .... my shoulder.
3 .... the end of time.
4 to go .... agonies.
5 .... a mistake.

Choose from these: until, for, without, over, in, out, through.

GRAMMAR

Who done it?

Things get done *by* people but *with* instruments. Sometimes *by* is used incorrectly, as in: 'The window was forced open by a screwdriver.' It might have been forced open *by* a burglar, but it was done *with* a screwdriver. If you are ever in doubt, just remember: 'The murder was done *by* a man *with* a gun.'

That sentence could have been taken from a 'whodunnit', that is a detective or murder mystery. A dictionary may say that the word is made up from 'who, done (vulg. pa.t. of do), it'. The abbreviations mean that done is regarded as a 'vulgar past tense of do'.

Perhaps readers who use *done* instead of *did*, as in 'I done it' or 'The lads done well', are cringing

with embarrassment? Cheer up! If you now look up 'vulgar', you will find that, although it means 'coarse or lacking good taste', it can also mean 'commonly used but incorrect'. Now, some linguists (people who study language) reckon that *most* native English-speakers (those whose first language is English) say 'I done it' — at least seven out of every ten of them. You might very well ask: 'If this is the case, why is it incorrect to do so?'

The answer is that it is not necessarily incorrect. Many dialects of English use this and similar phrases, such as 'Me and her went to the zoo' and 'them animals in that cage'. These would be wrong in what we call Standard English, which is spoken by perhaps three out of every ten people.

WEST INDIAN
She bin come home yesterday.
(*She came home yesterday.*)

WELSH
Have a tidy swill.
(*Have a good wash.*)

SCOTTISH
Do you need any messages?
(*Do you need any shopping?*)

IRISH
Would you be wanting something to eat?

THAMES ESTUARY
As we was walking down the street she said she ain't never seen him.

It is worth learning how to write Standard English even if you do not speak it, because to a large extent this is the English that is taught internationally — the English that is understood by everyone. Some regard it as only another dialect, the one spoken mainly by the so-called 'educated classes'.

More do's and don'ts in Standard English

There are some traditional rules of grammar that many adults were taught at school, but which are nonsense. Unfortunately, some adults (including possibly some teachers) still follow them. One is that you must not begin a sentence with 'and' or 'but' (these are 'conjunctions', or joining words). Another is that you should never split an 'infinitive' (verbs in the form of 'to go', 'to carry', etc).

To avoid using 'and' or 'but' at the start of a sentence is as much a superstition as not treading on the lines of the pavement. There is no reason why you should not use them, and every reason why you should whenever you find it necessary. Otherwise you will find yourself writing sentences that are too long, often stilted, and difficult to follow.

You won't find the need to split many infinitives, but when you do, go ahead. Don't be afraid to bravely go where others fear to tread. Very often splitting infinitives is sloppy. But sometimes there is no other place for a word but between the 'to' and the rest of the verb, as in: 'To really enjoy yourself, set out

early.' Here, 'really' cannot be placed anywhere else in the sentence, either at the beginning or after 'yourself'. You could write: 'If you really want to enjoy yourself, set out early'. But this does not have quite the same meaning.

Compare these two sentences and notice the difference in meaning:
I want you to *really* like her.
I *really* want you to like her.

Correct the following, where necessary, to give Standard English (answers on page 30):

1 That's another fine mess you've got me into.
2 For what are you blaming me for?
3 The race is now between the leading three.
4 Compared to English, French is easy to learn.
5 Finish them sandwiches before you start the ice-cream.
6 When you have done the front garden, make a start on the back.
7 They tried to quickly get there.
8 They made no effort to even get there on time.

6 Contradictory proverbs — It all depends on what you mean

A proverb is a popular saying that gives advice or a warning. Most proverbs are very old and pass on little nuggets of wisdom.

People use proverbs to make a point. But sometimes you can find two proverbs that seem to have completely opposite meanings.

Take, for example, these two well-known sayings: 'Too many cooks spoil the broth' and 'Many hands make light work'. They appear to be making completely opposite points. The first seems to say that if you have a lot of people trying to do the same job, they will get in each other's way and make a mess of it. The second suggests that a job will be all the easier if lots of people help.

But if we apply these proverbs to the right situation, they can both be good advice. In the first case – in a small kitchen, say — a number of people (cooks) might get in each other's way as they try to make the same pot of soup. In the second case — clearing up after a party, for example — the more people who help, the quicker the job will be done.

Here are two more proverbs that seem to contradict each other: 'Absence makes the heart grow fonder' and 'Out of sight, out of mind'. The first suggests that you think more lovingly about relatives or friends when you don't see them for a long time. The second implies that you forget them! Can they both be good proverbs? Think about it, and then see the answers (pages 30 and 31) for a possible explanation.

Many hands making work light

**See if you can complete the 'opposites' of the
following proverbs (answers on page 31):**

1 Never put off for tomorrow what can be done today. (More haste, less ...)

2 The early bird catches the worm. (Everything comes to him who ...)

3 Look before you leap. (He who hesitates ...)

4 Nothing ventured, nothing gained. (Better safe ...)

5 Sticks and stones may break my bones, but names will never hurt
   me. (The pen is mightier than ...)

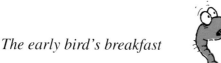

The early bird's breakfast

**Animal proverbs
Fill in the missing animal or word
(answers on page 31)**

1 The ..... can't change its spots.

2 When the ..... away, the .....will play

3 A ..... may look at a king.

4 You can't teach an old :.... new tricks.

5 Don't look a ..... horse in the mouth.

6 One ..... doesn't make a summer.

7 Don't count your ..... before they
  are hatched.

Don't look a ... horse in the mouth

Making a point

People use proverbs to make a point. But if proverbs are overused, they become tiresome. If, every time you opened your mouth to speak, an adult tried to shut you up with that most irritating of all proverbs, 'Children should be seen and not heard,' you might begin to think that proverbs are not all that they are cracked up to be. In the last century, children were expected to be silent in the presence of elders unless they were spoken to. Nowadays children have more freedom to express their views. In response to an adult's 'Children should be seen ...' you might try quoting a proverb from the Bible (Psalms of David): 'Out of the very mouths of babes and sucklings....' This means that the young and innocent sometimes come out with the wisest truths. On the other hand, if you deserve to be told off, you should remember the proverb, 'A still tongue makes a wise head'. In other words, you will learn more by listening than by talking!

Seen but not heard

Misunderstood proverbs

Some proverbs are misunderstood, and people use them for the wrong reasons. For example, 'Charity begins at home' should not be used as an excuse for not giving to those in need outside of your own family. It means that charity — kindness towards fellow human beings — is learnt at home when you are young.

Mixed-up proverbs

The following proverbs have been mixed up. See if you can unscramble them (answers on page 31):

1 Life is not all good memories.
2 A rich man's joke is a joy forever.
3 When in doubt, 'tis folly to be wise.
4 Liars should have beer and skittles.
5 A thing of beauty is always funny.
6 Where ignorance is bliss, do nowt.

Another misunderstood proverb is 'The exception proves the rule'. In this, 'proves' is an old use of the word and means 'tests'. The saying is not claiming that to prove a rule you need an exception, but that an exception highlights a rule. Some people trot this weary old proverb out whenever there is mention or an occurrence of an exception, like the sports commentator who complained: 'Rovers were poor today. Only Wright played well. He was the exception that proved the rule.' What rule?

The proverbial sick parrot

Have you noticed how people use the word 'proverbial' as an excuse for talking in clichés? 'I was as sick as the proverbial parrot.' There isn't a proverb about a sick parrot. It's just a saying, 'as sick as a parrot', and certainly does not impart any wisdom.

Another example is: 'We were up with the proverbial lark.' This is just an excuse for using the cliché, 'up with the lark' — or is the proverbial lark 'the early bird that catches the worm'?

At any rate, 'proverbial' has now come to be used in this other sense, to mean 'well known' or 'as in the well-known saying'. People using it in this way are more or less saying 'It's OK to talk in clichés, if you signal the fact'!

This is a good example of how English changes — a new meaning is given to an old word.

Polly's poorly

Answers

1 What's the point? (page 4)

After all, if you wrote without spaces between words, for example, it would be very difficult for the reader to follow, wouldn't it?

Commas (page 5)

1 *Jack, my youngest brother, has just started school.*
2 *Schoolteacher Hilary Humperdinck was arrested for dangerous driving.*
3 *The race was sponsored by, but not connected with, the department store.*
4 *As soon as the rain started, up went the umbrellas.*
5 *The primary colours are red, blue, and yellow. (You could take the last comma out.)*
6 *You heard me calling, but you did not answer.*
7 *The senator, born in Orlando, Florida, of poor parents, supported the scheme.*
8 *The hand that rocks the cradle rules the world.*
9 *Having had lunch, I went back to my office.*
10 *'Here I am,' Tom replied. (OK)*

Compound words (page 7)

1 *fire/place*
2 *hope/full ('full' has become 'ful')*
3 *wave/length*
4 *trade/mark*
5 *country/side*
6 *work/man/like*
7 *extra/ordinary*
8 *super/natural*
9 *king/dom ('-dom' is not a word, but a suffix, something placed at the end of a word. It means 'dominion')*
10 *bi/cycle ('bi-' is not a word, but a prefix, something placed at the beginning. It means 'two')*
11 *mother/hood (-hood is a suffix meaning a state or condition: manhood)*
12 *waste/paper*
13 *news/letter*
14 *rain/storm*
15 *hog/wash*
16 *hand/saw*
17 *bed/spread*
18 *motor/boat*
19 *night/dress*
20 *over/print*
21 *pent/house (pent comes from an Old French word meaning 'appendage' or*

addition to')
22 *when/so/ever*
23 *type/writer*
24 *yester/day ('yester' — an Old English word for 'preceding')*

It's right, its wrong (page 8)
1,2 and 3 are wrong — they should all be 'it's'.

Misplaced apostrophes (page 8)
1 *That's my sister's poem.*
2 *You'll let me know, won't you?*
3 *Is that ball yours? (no apostrophe)*
4 *No, it's Jones's.*
5 *Yours sincerely.*
6 *Women's rights.*
7 *The men's room.*
8 *It's a hard life.*
9 *I didn't want to do it.*
10 *Aren't you lucky?*

2 Misprints (page 10)
1 *muslin (muslim)*
2 *boar (bore)*
3 *tugs (thugs)*
4 *goods (good)*
5 *foot (fool)*
6 *water (waiter)*
7 *cock (clock)*
8 *crowd (crow)*
9 *reception (deception)*
10 *Satan (satin)*
11 *visible (risible)*
12 *pricked (picked)*

3 How not to spell potatoe (page 11)
The three spelling mistakes:
'sentance' should be 'sentence', 'seperate' should be 'separate' and 'mispellings' should be 'misspellings'.

Sounds the same (page 11)
*The word is **'cite'** and it means 'to call or summon'.*

Pairs of homophones (pages 11 and 12)
1 *A ring, **B** wring.*
2 *A reign, **B** rain, **C** rein.*
3 *A sum, **B** some.*
4 *A dear, **B** deer.*
5 *A eight, **B** ate.*
6 *A quire, **B** choir.*
7 *A banned, **B** band.*
8 *A wood, **B** would.*
9 *A bear, **B** bare.*
10 *A boy, **B** buoy.*
11 *A dye, **B** die.*
12 *A quay, **B** key.*

13 *A ruff, **B** rough.*
14 *A cue, **B** queue.*
15 *A colonel, **B** kernel.*
16 *A plain, **B** plane.*
17 *A fur, **B** fir.*
18 *A none, **B** nun.*
19 *A right, **B** write,*
    *C rite, **D** wright.*
20 *A peer, **B** pier.*
21 *A lynx, **B** links.*
22 *A aisle, **B** isle.*
23 *A cent, **B** scent.*
24 *A here, **B** hear.*
25 *A toad, **B** towed.*

There is no such word as 'playwrite', but a person who writes plays is called a 'playwright'.

Spelling rules
(page 13)
1 *Deceit.* **2** *Achieve (correct).*
3 *Seeing (correct).* **4** *Their.*
5 *Weir (another exception).*
6 *Cashier.* **7** *Cavalier (correct).*
8 *Musketeer.* **9** *Sieve (correct).*
10 *Seismic (correct, different sound as in 'size').*
11 *Retriever.* **12** *Shriek.*

Plurals
(page 14)
1 *banjoes or banjos (both accepted).* **2** *mosquitoes or mosquitos (both accepted).*
3 *cargoes.* **4** *dynamos.* **5** *haloes or halos (both accepted).*
6 *mottoes or mottos.*
7 *tornadoes.* **8** *tomatoes.*
9 *sopranos.* **10** *volcanoes.*
11 *echoes.* **12** *ratios.*

Misspellings corrected
(page 15)
1 *abbreviate (correct)*
2 *abscess*
3 *abyss (correct)*
4 *accelerate*
5 *accommodate*
6 *acquire (correct)*
7 *address*
8 *allotted (correct)*
9 *anoint*
10 *arctic*
11 *assassin*
12 *bargain*
13 *barley*
14 *braggadocio (correct)*
15 *broccoli*
16 *bulrush*
17 *calendar*
18 *caress (correct)*
19 *catarrh*
20 *cauliflower (correct)*
21 *chihuahua (correct)*
22 *colloquial (correct)*
23 *colonnade*
24 *colossal*
25 *concede*
26 *conscience (correct)*
27 *dachshund*

ADRESS

28

28 *deciduous (correct)*
29 *delicatessen*
30 *desiccate*
31 *diarrhoea*
32 *dinghy (correct)*
33 *ecstasy*
34 *eczema (correct)*
35 *embarrass*
36 *Fahrenheit*
37 *fidgeting*
38 *flight*
39 *focussed or focused*
40 *fuselage (correct)*
41 *gaseous*
42 *gaiety*
43 *grammar*
44 *grievous*
45 *gymkhana*
46 *handkerchief*
47 *harass*
48 *herbaceous*
49 *hundredth*
50 *hypocrisy*
51 *immobile*
52 *impresario*
53 *indefensible*
54 *innocuous*
55 *innuendo*
56 *intercede*
57 *interrogate*
58 *irascible*
59 *iridescent*
60 *isosceles*
61 *jodhpurs*
62 *khaki*
63 *kitchen*
64 *lacquer*
65 *lasso*

66 *liaise*
67 *liquefy*
68 *loquacious*
69 *mayonnaise*
70 *millennium*
71 *misspelled (or misspelt)*
72 *moccasin*
73 *monastery*
74 *niece*
75 *nuclear*
76 *occurred*
77 *odyssey*
78 *paraffin (or paraffine)*
79 *pavilion (correct)*
80 *preference*
81 *propeller*
82 *questionnaire*
83 *rarefy*
84 *renaissance*
85 *resurrection*
86 *saccharin (saccharine)*
87 *sacrilegious*
88 *sandwich (correct)*
89 *sapphire*
90 *satisfactory*
91 *saxophone*
92 *specimen*
93 *spherical*
94 *supersede*
95 *symmetry*
96 *temporary*
97 *tomato*
98 *tyranny*
99 *vermilion*
100 *yacht*

TOMATOE

How many did you get right ?

4 Is that really what they said? (page 17)

1 *Let there be light.*
2 *When shall we three meet again ...?*
3 *By the shore of Gitche Gumee.*
4 *Workers of the world unite.*
5 *I don't want to belong to any club that will have me as a member.*
6 *The report of my death was an exaggeration.*
7 *Dr Livingstone, I presume.*
8 *If you can meet with Triumph and Disaster and treat those two impostors just the same*
9 *Tiger! Tiger! burning bright in the forests of the night.*
10 *The law is a ass.*
11 *Water, water, everywhere, Nor any drop to drink.*
12 *They shall grow not old, as we that are left grow old.*
13 *I like to be alone.*
14 *Play it Sam. Play 'As time goes by'.* (Ingrid Bergman in the film *Casablanca*.)

5 Rules? Ignore them!
Find the preposition (page 19)

1 *In* a mess.
2 *Over* my shoulder.
3 *Until* the end of time.

4 *To go **through** agonies.*
5 ***without** a mistake.*

Standard English (page 21)

1 *That's another fine mess you've got me into.(OK. '... into which you've got me' is awkward.)*
2 *What are you blaming me for?*
3 *The race is now between the leading three. (OK)*
4 *Compared with English, French is easy to learn.*
5 *Finish those sandwiches before you start the ice-cream.('... them sandwiches' is commonly used but is not Standard English.)*
6 *When you have done the front garden, make a start on the back. (OK)*
7 *They tried to get there quickly.*
8 *They made no effort to even get there on time. (OK. You could 'unsplit' the infinitive by moving 'even' in front of 'to' or to the end of the sentence, but it reads more comfortably where it is.)*

6 It all depends . . . contradictory proverbs (page 22)

Absence makes the heart grow fonder' is similar to the proverb

'Familiarity breeds contempt', which means that, if you see too much of someone, you might begin to take them for granted, perhaps magnify their faults and lose respect for them. But if that person is not there, perhaps has gone away for a few months, you might forget their faults. 'Out of sight, out of mind' means that anyone who is not around runs the risk of being forgotten. So the first applies more to absent close friends or family, the second to someone who might be overlooked for promotion at work, say, or inclusion in a team. In other words, if they fail to show their talents, they will be forgotten.

Opposites (page 23)

1 *More haste, less **speed**.*
2 *Everything comes to him who **waits**.*
3 *He who hesitates **is lost**.*
4 *Better safe **than sorry**.*
5 *The pen is mightier than **the sword**.*

Animal proverbs (page 23)

1 *The **leopard** can't change its spots.*
2 *When the **cat's** away, the **mice** will play.*
3 *A **cat** may look at a king.*
4 *You can't teach an old **dog** new tricks.*
5 *Don't look a **gift** horse in the mouth.*
6 *One **swallow** doesn't make a summer.*
7 *Don't count your **chickens** before they are hatched.*

Mixed-up proverbs (page 24)

1 *Life is not all beer and skittles.*
2 *A rich man's joke is always funny.*
3 *When in doubt, do nowt.*
4 *Liars should have good memories.*
5 *A thing of beauty is a joy forever.*
6 *Where ignorance is bliss, 'tis folly to be wise.*

Standard English is the speech or 'dialect' of the upper and upper-middle classes. It is normally used in writing English and teaching it to foreigners.